THE SECRET

Discovering God's Secret of Handling Money
(For Children Ages 8 - 12)

MOODY PUBLISHERS
CHICAGO

Leader's Guide

TABLE OF CONTENTS

Contents   **Pages**

✓ **Information Leaders Need to Know**

    Course Objectives / Leader's Responsibilities 3

    Information Leaders Need to Know 4-6

    What to Do Before the First Class 7

    Prayer List 8

    Loving the Students 9

✓ **Chapter Guides** 11-53

✓ **How to Conduct the Study**

    ■ One-on-One 55

    ■ In a Small Group 57,58

    ■ In Sunday School 59,60

    ■ In School 61,62

    ■ Quizzes 63-86

✓ **Prayer Lists** .... Unnumbered

© Copyright 1997 by Compass—Finances God's Way, Inc..

Unless otherwise notes, Scripture quotations are taken from the *New American Stand Bible*®, copyright 1960, 1962, 1963, 1968, 1971, 1972, 1973, 1975, 1977 by the Lockman Foundation. Used by permission.

Verses identified as NIV are taken from the *Holy Bible: New International Version*®, copyright 1973, 1978, 1984, by the International Bible Society. Used by permission of Zondervan Bible Publishers

Verses identified as LB are taken from *The Living Bible*, 1971 by Tyndale House Publishers. Used by permission.

Verses identified as KJV are taken from the King James Version.

ISBN-13 978-0-8024-3153-0   *Printed in the United States of America*   5 7 9 10 8 6 4

STUDY OBJECTIVES / LEADER'S RESPONSIBILITIES

1. **Objectives of the Study**

   ✓ **Encourage the students to experience more intimate fellowship with Christ.**

   Luke 16:11 expresses the correlation between how we handle our resources and the quality of our fellowship with the Lord: *"If therefore you have not been faithful in the use of worldly wealth, who will entrust the true riches to you?"* For some students, this study may be their first opportunity to learn about Jesus Christ.

   ✓ **Challenge each person to invite Jesus Christ to be their Lord.**

   We believe money is a primary competitor with Christ for the lordship of our lives. Matthew 6:24 reads, *"No man can serve two masters, you will love one and hate the other . . . you cannot serve God and Mammon* [money].*"*

   ✓ **Provide children ages 8-12 with a basic knowledge of God's principles of handling money.**

   The study is designed to teach and help children apply foundational financial principles from God's Word.

2. **The Primary Responsibilities of the Leader**

   ✓ **Unconditionally love and encourage your students.**
   Children are more receptive to spiritual truth when they have been loved. They want to know how much you care before they care how much you know.

   ✓ **Hold your students accountable to complete the assignments.**
   Be a model of faithfulness. Luke 6:40 reads, *"Everyone, after he has been fully trained, will be like his teacher."* The leader must be faithful in every area. Always arrive early, pray consistently for your students, know the memory verses fluently, and be well prepared for each class.

   ✓ **Conform to the Compass procedure of leading the study.**

INFORMATION LEADERS NEED TO KNOW

1. **This study for children ages 8-12 is designed to be taught in a variety of settings:** one-on-one, in a small group, in a Sunday school class, and in a Christian school or home school environment.

   In the Leader's Guide are clear directions for how the study should be taught in each of these settings.

2. **How does a leader become qualified to lead the study?**

   Leader training is not required for the *Secret of Handling Money God's Way* study. This teacher's guide provides the information needed to lead this study in your group. Should you have any questions regarding this study, you may contact us at 1-800-525-7000 or visit us online at compass1.org for assistance.

3. **The leader is the key.**

   For the study to be successful, the leader must be prepared. Use illustrations and examples the children can understand and will find interesting to "bring to life" the Lord's financial principles. The leader should be creative, use humor and love the students. Make it interesting and fun.

4. **The Leader's Guide is divided into four sections:**

   ✓ **Information leaders need to know.** The leaders should carefully study pages 3 through 9 before leading the class.

   ✓ **The chapter guides.** There is a guide for each chapter that contains the answers for the questions. The guides are found on pages 10 through 53.

   ✓ **How to conduct the study.** This section addresses how the study should be taught in different settings: one-on-one (page 55), in a small group (pages 57 and 58), in Sunday school (pages 59 and 60), and in a Christian school or home school (pages 61 and 62).

   ✓ **Prayer List.** Read more about the Prayer List on page 8.

5. **Student Requirements**

   Before each class the students are required to read a chapter, memorize a scripture, complete a practical exercise called "Work It Out!" and answer the assigned questions.

6. **The classes are designed to meet for approximately 50 minutes.** The teacher may elect to alter this time.

7. **Size of the Classes**

   If you are teaching the study in a small group setting, we suggest no more than eight students in the group. In a Sunday school or Christian school there is no class size limitation.

8. **What age is this study designed for?**

   The study is designed for eight to twelve-year-olds. If you have a group of both younger and older children, it is suggested that the group be divided according to age. This allows the experience and comprehension level to be similar in each group.

9. **Parental Involvement**

   Whenever possible, encourage parents to be involved in helping their children with this study.

10. **Evangelism**

    Many people are introduced to Jesus Christ as their Savior when they are young. At the end of Chapter 9 there is a section describing how a child can come to know Christ. Leaders should use this opportunity to share how the children can come to know the Savior.

11. **How to Place an Order**

    Should you wish to receive additional materials, you may:

    ✓ **Write Compass:** Send your order and check to: Compass-Finances God's Way, PO Box 2557, Sanford, FL 32772-2557. Be sure to give us your street address.

    ✓ **Use the Compass Web Site:** www.compass1.org.

    ✓ **Call Compass** at (407) 331-6000 to place an order.

    ✓ Please order three weeks in advance to insure a timely delivery. A new order form is enclosed with each shipment of materials.

12. **Promoting Financial Products or Services**

    No one may use their affiliation with Compass—Finances God's Way to promote or influence the sale of any investments, financial services, or professional services.

13. **Other Compass Studies.**

    ✓ *The ABCs of Handling Money God's Way* **for children 7 and younger**

    ✓ *Give, Save & Spend* **for high school students**

    ✓ *Give, Save & Spend* **for college students**

    ✓ The *Navigating Your Finances God's Way* **adult small group study**

    ✓ *Money and Marriage God's Way*

    ✓ *Business God's Way*

14. **More about Compass**

    Compass is an interdenominational ministry that trains people to apply biblical financial principles to their lives. Compass is a non-profit organization. It is governed by a Board of Directors, none of whom receive a salary from serving the ministry.

WHAT TO DO BEFORE THE FIRST CLASS

Meet with the students before the first class to begin to love them and communicate the following:

1. **Review the students' requirements.**

The requirements for each chapter are designed to take approximately thirty minutes outside of class. If for any reason a child comes to the class unprepared, they will not be allowed to participate in the discussion. The student requirements are found at the top of page 5 of this Leader's Guide. It is especially important to review these requirements.

2. **Describe the other important "ground rules":**

   ✓ The class opens and closes in prayer.

   ✓ Scriptures are memorized in the version used in *The Secret* and not in another version of the Bible.

   ✓ The classes start and stop on time.

   ✓ Although the class will be fun, nobody should interrupt while the leader or another student is talking.

3. **Dispense the materials.**

Each student should have his or her own copy of *The Secret.*

4. **Assign Chapter 1.**

The student should read Chapter 1 and complete the questions, memorize *Luke 16:11,* and get a Bible if they do not already have one.

PRAYER LIST

To help the children develop a more consistent prayer life, we use the prayer list.

✓ In a class that has more than eight students, divide the children into prayer groups of no more than seven or eight. Then toward the end of each class, ask the children to gather with their group to take prayer requests and share any answers to prayer. Students should stay in the same group during the entire study.

✓ During the first meeting, have each child tell the others in their group the information asked for at the top of the prayer list — their name, phone number, etc.

✓ One prayer list should be filled out for each child in a group. The prayer lists are located in the back of *The Secret*.

✓ **Ask the children to complete their own prayer list before coming to class to save time.** Each child is encouraged to pray daily for every child in their group during the study.

Examine the sample prayer list below.

PRAYER LIST

Name: Mary Johnson
Telephone: 555-9876
Home Address: 321 Victor Ave.
Orlando, FL 32750

School: _____
Age: _____
Parents: George and Jane

Chapter	Pray For Me	Answers To Prayer
1	For Tommy to get over the flu and for Ann, a neighbor, to come to Christ.	
2	For Tommy to do well in reading and for Ann to come to know the Lord.	Tommy completely well.
3	For a safe family vacation and for Ann to know the Lord.	Tommy reading well.
4		
5		

LOVING THE STUDENTS

One of the primary responsibilities of the leader is to love the students. Remember, children want to know how much you care before they care how much you know.

The leader needs to grasp every opportunity to love the students both inside and outside of the class.

1. Love the students outside of class.

    - We suggest that the leaders contact each student once or twice during the study to encourage and love them. The contacts may be by telephone, by mail, or in person. **Be sure to get the parents' permission before initiating any contact with the students.**

    - Consider organizing a social event for the children. This might be a dessert get-together, a picnic, or any other relaxed setting that encourages the development of relationships.

    - It is greatly encouraging to do something special as a "graduation" gift when the study is completed. The following are suggestions:

        - Take a photograph of the class and give it to the children.

        - Present a graduation certificate.

        - Hold a social event to celebrate graduation.

2. Love the children inside of class.

    - The leader's attitude should be humble and caring — not a critical or a "know-it-all" attitude. We are students among students, in that we all are growing in understanding the unfathomable Word of God.

    - After a child answers a question, encourage, affirm and thank them.

    - If an answer is incorrect, be careful not to discourage the child by responding harshly or negatively.

    - Maintain good eye contact and be attentive. We communicate through our body language.

GRANDPA AND ABIGAIL
Leader's Guide for Chapter 1

Compass's overview of Chapter 1: The primary objectives for the first class are to begin to develop close relationships among the children (if there is more than one student), to reinforce the study requirements, and to learn some of the basic issues of what the Bible says about money.

Note: The blank space following most agenda numbers is for the leader to fill in the scheduled time. For example, if your class begins at 7:00, #2 would read 7:00, #4 would read 7:05 and so forth. This is designed to help the leader monitor the time so the class will end punctually.

Agenda:

1. Open in prayer.

2. _____ (5 minutes) Have everyone recite from memory:

> *"If therefore you have not been faithful in the use of worldly wealth*, who will entrust the true riches to you?"* (Luke 16:11).

3. Confirm that everyone has a Bible and knows there are 66 books in the Bible.

4. _____ (30 minutes) Begin the **Answer These Questions!** discussion.

1 Open the Bible and read *Isaiah 55:8-9*. Do you think God's way of handling money is different from the way most people handle money?

Note: Compass's comments, in brackets, will follow each question. Following Compass's comments there will be a space for the leader's answer.

[God's principles are entirely different from the principles people use to manage their money.]

2 What do you think would be the greatest difference?

[Most people do not believe the Lord plays a personal role in finances, but Scripture reveals He has the major role.]

3 There are more than 2,350 verses in the Bible that talk about money. Why do you think the Lord says so much about money?

[The Lord knew money would be a big part of our lives, so He wanted us to know how to handle money wisely.]

4 Look up and read *Luke 16:11*. What do you think are the "true riches" the Lord mentions in this verse?

[The true riches are a closer relationship with Jesus Christ.]

Remaining agenda:

1. _____ (5 minutes) Review what the students are required to do for the next chapter:

   - Answer the questions on pages 19 to 21.
   - Memorize *1 Chronicles 29:11-12*.
   - Read Chapter 2 — A Giant in the Clubhouse.
   - Complete the **Work It Out!** assignment of writing down how much money they receive and spend for the week.

2. _____ (10 minutes) Complete the Prayer Lists. If the class is larger than eight, divide into groups of no more than eight. Each participant should have one Prayer List for each person in his or her group, including himself or herself. Take prayer requests and note them on the Prayer Lists.

3. End in prayer.

A GIANT IN THE CLUBHOUSE
Leader's Guide for Chapter 2

Compass's overview of Chapter 2: In many respects this is the most important chapter, because the remainder of the study builds upon understanding the part God has in handling money. The Lord's ownership of all things is foundational.

Agenda:

1. Open in prayer.

2. _____ (5 minutes) Have everyone recite from memory:

"Everything in the heavens and earth is yours, O Lord, and this is your kingdom. We adore you as being in control of everything. Riches and honor come from you alone, and you are the Ruler of all mankind; your hand controls power and might, and it is at your discretion that men are made great and given strength" (1 Chronicles 29:11-12, LB).

3. Confirm that each student wrote down how much money they received and spent last week.

4. _____ (30 minutes) Begin group discussion of **Answer These Questions!**

1 Read *1 Corinthians 10:26*. Who owns everything in the world?

[The Lord owns everything in the world.]

2 Name some of your things that God owns.

3   Read *1 Chronicles 29:11-12*. Who controls everything that happens?

[The Lord is in control of all circumstances.]

4   List the things people need to live a normal life.

[Food, clothing, and a place to live]

5   Read *Matthew 6:31-33* and *Philippians 4:19*. What do these verses say about God taking care of your needs?

[God has promised to provide our needs if we seek first the kingdom of God and His righteousness, in other words, if we put the Lord first.]

6 Give an example from the Bible of the Lord providing for someone's needs.

[The Lord gave Israel manna in the wilderness; Jesus fed five thousand; and the Lord sent ravens to feed Elijah.]

7 What was the most interesting thing you learned from reading this chapter?

Remaining agenda:

1. _____ (5 minutes) Review what the students are required to do for the next chapter.

- ✓ Read Chapter 3 — Fixing the Fence.
- ✓ Answer the Questions on pages 27 to 29.
- ✓ Memorize *1 Corinthians 4:2*.
- ✓ Complete the **Work It Out!** exercise. Get three jars, cans or boxes and label one GIVING, one SAVING and one SPENDING. For the next two weeks write down how much you put in the GIVING, SPENDING and SAVING jars when you receive money.

2. _____ (10 minutes) Note on the Prayer Lists requests and answers to prayers.
3. End in prayer.

FIXING THE FENCE
Leader's Guide for Chapter 3

Compass's overview of Chapter 3: We have the responsibility to be faithful stewards of the things God gives us, and the Lord will hold us accountable for how we handle them.

Agenda:

1. Open in prayer.

2. _____ (5 minutes) Have everyone recite from memory:

"Moreover it is required in stewards, that a man be found faithful" (1 Corinthians 4:2, KJV).

3. Confirm that everyone secured three jars, cans or boxes and labeled one GIVING, one SAVING and one SPENDING. Also confirm that they are writing down how much they are putting into each container when they receive money.

4. _____ (30 minutes) Begin the discussion of **Answer These Questions!**

1 Look up the word *steward* in the dictionary. What does it mean?

[A steward is a manager of someone else's property.]

2 Read *1 Corinthians 4:2*. According to this verse, what are stewards required to do?

[Stewards are to be *faithful*.]

3 Look up *Luke 16:10.* Why do you think it is important to be faithful with small things?

[If a person is unfaithful in a little thing, he or she will be unfaithful in a large matter.]

4 Read *Luke 16:1-2.* Why did the master remove the unfaithful steward from his job?

[The steward was removed because he wasted the master's things.]

5 Read *Hebrews 4:13*. Does the Lord see everything you do? How will knowing this help you change any of the ways you act or spend money?

6 Read *2 Corinthians 5:9-10*. What will happen to us in the future? Why is this important for us to understand?

Remaining agenda:

1. _____ (5 minutes) Review what the students are required to do for the next chapter.

   ✔ Read Chapter 4 — The Oil Didn't Stop.

   ✔ Answer the Questions on pages 36 and 37

   ✔ Memorize *Proverbs 22:7*.

   ✔ Complete **Work It Out!** List any money they owe and to whom they owe money. Then have them describe how they plan to pay it back.

2. _____ (10 minutes) Note in the Prayer Lists requests and answers to prayers.

3. End in prayer.

THE OIL DIDN'T STOP
Leader's Guide for Chapter 4

Compass's overview of Chapter 4: Debt is a struggle for many people. It is consistently discouraged in Scripture. Challenge the students to establish the goal of staying debt free.

Agenda:

1. Open in prayer.

2. _____ (5 minutes) Have the children recite from memory:

"Just as the rich rule the poor, so the borrower is servant to the lender" (Proverbs 22:7, LB).

3. Confirm that everyone has completed the **Work It Out!** exercise, listing what they owe and describing how they plan to pay it back.

4. _____ (35 minutes) Begin the discussion of **Answer These Questions!**

1 How does the dictionary define *debt*?

[Debt is when we owe money.]

2 When someone pays interest on debt, what do you think that means?

[Interest is the extra money you pay when you borrow money.]

3   Why do you think most people go into debt?

[Many people go into debt to buy things right away. They are not patient to save enough money to buy things with cash.]

4   Read *Romans 13:8*. What does this verse say about owing money?

[We are encouraged to stay out of debt.]

5   Read *Proverbs 22:7*. What does this verse say about someone who borrows money?

6 Why do you think the Lord wants us to stay out of debt?

[He wants us to get out of debt so we won't be slaves to people; rather we can be free to serve the Lord.]

Remaining agenda:

1. (5 minutes) Review what the students are required to do for the next chapter.

    - ✓ Read Chapter 5 — The Big Day.
    - ✓ Answer the Questions on pages 44 and 45.
    - ✓ Memorize *Proverbs 12:15*.
    - ✓ Complete **Work It Out!** Make a list of the people who will be good counselors. Write down at least one question to ask each of them about money.

2. (10 minutes) Note in the Prayer Lists requests and answers to prayer.

3. End in prayer.

Reminder for leaders: Encourage your students to continue to think about *1 Chronicles 29:11-12* to more consistently recognize the part God plays with money.

THE BIG DAY
Leader's Guide for Chapter 5

Compass's overview of Chapter 5: Everyone should seek counsel when they need to make decisions. Our culture discourages people from seeking counsel.

Remember to illustrate each major principle with a brief story your students can understand.

Agenda:

1. Open in prayer.

2. _____ (5 minutes) Have the children recite from memory:

"The way of a fool is right in his own eyes, but a wise man is he who listens to counsel" (Proverbs 12:15).

3. Confirm that everyone has completed the **Work It Out!** exercise, making a list of counselors and the questions to ask each of them about money.

4. _____ (30 minutes) Begin the discussion of the **Answer These Questions!**

1 What does it mean to seek counsel or advice?

[To seek counsel is to ask another person for their ideas.]

2 Are there reasons why you do not ask for advice? If there are, please list them.

[Many people are afraid to ask for advice.]

3 What are some of the good things you have learned from seeking counsel?

4 Read *Psalm 16:7* and *Psalm 32:8*. What are some of the ways the Lord counsels us?

[The Lord counsels us primarily through prayer, the Bible, godly people and our parents.]

5 Read *Psalm 119:105, 2 Timothy 3:16-17* and *Hebrews 4:12*. Each of these verses tells us something about the Scriptures. Write what each verse says in the space below.

Psalm 119:105 — [The Bible helps guide our path.]

2 Timothy 3:16-17 — [God gave us the scriptures to train and equip us for godly living.]

Hebrews 4:12 — [The Word of God is alive and is able to judge our thoughts and intentions.]

6 Why do you think you should avoid the counsel of wicked people?

Remaining agenda:

1. _____ (5 minutes) Review what the students are required to do for the next chapter.

   - Read Chapter 6 — Honest in Small Things.
   - Answer the Questions on pages 53 and 54.
   - Memorize *Leviticus 19:11*.
   - Complete the **Work It Out!** exercise. Make a list of the things they want to buy, how much they will cost, and how they plan to save enough money to buy them.

2. _____ (5 minutes) Note on the Prayer Lists requests and answers to prayers.

3. End in prayer.

HONEST IN SMALL THINGS
Leader's Guide for Chapter 6

Compass's overview of Chapter 6: Dishonest practices are common, but the Lord demands that His children act with total honesty and integrity. This section is one of the most challeng-ing of the entire study.

Agenda:

1. Open in prayer.

2. _____ (5 minutes) Have the children recite from memory:

> "You shall not steal, nor deal falsely, nor lie to one another" (Leviticus 19:11).

3. Confirm that everyone has completed the **Work It Out!** exercise of reviewing the things they want to buy, how much they cost, and how they plan on saving enough to buy them.

4. _____ (30 minutes) Begin the discussion of **Answer These Questions!**

1 Read *Leviticus 19:11* and *Exodus 20:15*. According to these verses, what does the Lord say about being honest?

[The Lord wants us to be honest all the time.]

2 Look up *Luke 16:10*. Why do you think Jesus said we should be honest in small things?

[He knew if we were not honest with small things, we would not be honest with bigger things.]

3 Are you always honest — even in small things?

4 If you are not always honest, what will you do to change?

5 Look up the word *restitution* in the dictionary. How would you define it?

[Restitution involves the return of what was gotten dishonestly, plus some extra.]

6 What should you do if you took something dishonestly?

[Ask forgiveness from the Lord and make restitution.]

7 What was the most important thing you learned from reading this chapter?

Remind the Students:

When you become a teenager, we recommend that you enroll in the Compass *Give, Save & Spend* study for high school students. The study will help you with the money issues you will face at that stage of your life.

Remaining agenda:

1. _____ (5 minutes) Review what the students are required to do for the next chapter.

   ✓ Read Chapter 7 — Midnight.

   ✓ Answer the Questions on pages 62 and 63.

   ✓ Memorize *Acts 20:35*.

   ✓ Complete the **Work It Out!** exercise, making a list of whom they want to give to and how much they want to give.

2. _____ (10 minutes) Note in the Prayer Lists requests and answers to prayers.

3. End in prayer.

MIDNIGHT
Leader's Guide for Chapter 7

Compass's overview of Chapter 7: Communicate to the students the importance of giving with the proper attitude and how this can bring us closer to Christ.

Agenda:

1. Open in prayer.

2. _____ (5 minutes) Have the children recite from memory:

> "... remember the words of the Lord Jesus, that He Himself said, 'It is more blessed to give than to receive'" (Acts 20:35).

3. Confirm that everyone made a list of whom they want give to and how much they want to give.

4. _____ (30 minutes) Begin the discussion of **Answer These Questions!**

1 The Lord says it is important to give with the right attitude. Look up *1 Corinthians 13:3* and *2 Corinthians 9:7*. According to these verses, what attitudes should we have when we give?

1 Corinthians 13:3 — [Giving without love is of no value to the giver.]

2 Corinthians 9:7 — [Do not give grudgingly or under compulsion, but rather cheerfully. The proper attitude is really important.]

30

2 How do you think you can learn to give cheerfully and from a heart filled with love?

[Give each gift to Jesus as a way of thanking Him for loving you and taking care of you.]

3 Do you think it is better to give a gift or receive a gift? Why?

Look up *Acts 20:35*. How do you think the Lord would answer this question?

[The Lord tells us it is more blessed to give than to receive. Most people think it is better to receive.]

4 List the benefits to the giver found in *Proverbs 11:24-25* and *Matthew 6:20*.

Proverbs 11:24-25 — [There is a material increase — in the Lord's time and way — to the giver.]

Matthew 6:20 — [We can lay up treasures in heaven, which we will enjoy for all eternity.]

5 Look up the word *tithe* in the dictionary. What does it mean to tithe?
[It means to give ten percent of our income.]

6 How much of your income do you give?

7 Do you think it is important to give to your church? Why?

8 Look up *Proverbs 28:27* and *Matthew 25:34-45*. What do these passages say about giving to the poor?

Proverbs 28:27 — [A person who gives to the poor will not be in need, but someone who doesn't give to the poor will be afflicted.]

Matthew 25:34-45 — [When we give to the poor we are giving to Christ Himself. When we do not give to the poor, we are not giving to Christ, and He is left hungry and naked.]

Remaining agenda:

1. _____ (5 minutes) Review what the students are required to do for the next chapter.

   - ✓ Read Chapter 8 — Just Like Nehemiah.
   - ✓ Answer the Questions on pages 70 and 71.
   - ✓ Memorize *Colossians 3:23-24*.
   - ✓ Review the **Work It Out!** exercise of writing a list of jobs they could do to earn money. They should describe how they should dress and what they should say when they go to ask for a job. Then they should try to get a job..

2. _____ (10 minutes) Note in the Prayer List requests and answers to prayers.

3. End in prayer.

JUST LIKE NEHEMIAH
Leader's Guide for Chapter 8

Compass's overview of Chapter 8: Work can be fulfilling or frustrating. Our job satisfaction depends upon understanding the Lord's perspective of work.

Agenda:

1. Open in prayer.

2. _____ (5 minutes) Have everyone recite from memory:

> *"Whatever you do, do your work heartily, as for the Lord rather than for men . . . It is the Lord Christ whom you serve"* (Colossians 3:23-24).

3. Confirm that everyone has completed making a list of jobs they can do, described how they would dress and what they would say when applying for a job, and what jobs they were able to get.

4. _____ (30 minutes) Begin the discussion of the **Answer These Questions!**

1 God plays a role in your work. Look up *Genesis 39:2-5, Exodus 36:1-2* and *Psalm 75:6-7*. What do each of these verses tell us about how the Lord is involved in work?

Genesis 39:2-5 — [The Lord is in control of success.]

Exodus 36:1-2 — [The Lord gives us our skills and understanding.]

Psalm 75:6-7 — [The Lord controls promotion.]

2 Do you think most people understand the Lord is so involved in their work? Why?

[No, most people don't recognize that the Lord plays any role in work, because He has chosen to be invisible.]

3 Read *Proverbs 6:6-11* and *2 Thessalonians 3:7-10*. What do these passages say about working hard?

Proverbs 6:6-11 — [The ant is honored as a hard worker.]

2 Thessalonians 3:7-10 — [If a person chooses not to work, we are not to feed them.]

4 Do you work hard at home and school? If you don't, what will you do to change?

5 Carefully study *Colossians 3:22-25*. Who do you really work for? Now that you understand this truth, how will it change your work habits?

Remaining agenda:

1. _____ (5 minutes) Review what the students are required to do for the next chapter.

   - Read Chapter 9 — Small Yet Wise.
   - Answer the Questions on pages 78 and 79.
   - Memorize *Proverbs 21:20* and *Proverbs 21:5*.
   - Review the **Work It Out!** exercise of opening a savings account and finding out what rate of interest they will earn on their savings.

2. _____ (10 minutes) Note in the Prayer Lists requests and answers to prayers.

3. End in prayer.

SMALL YET WISE
Leader's Guide for Chapter 9

Compass's overview of Chapter 9: This chapter's objective is to make the students aware of the scriptural principles for saving. Leaders must not recommend any specific investments, financial products, or services. Compass—Finances God's Way assumes no liability for any actions that students may take in relation to specific invest-ments or savings.

Agenda:

1. Open in prayer.

2. _____ (5 minutes) Have everyone recite from memory:

> *"The wise man saves for the future, but the foolish man spends whatever he gets"* (Proverbs 21: 20, LB).
>
> *"Steady plodding brings prosperity; hasty speculation brings poverty"* (Proverbs 21: 5, LB).

3. Confirm that everyone has completed the **Work It Out!** exercise of opening their savings account and finding out the interest rate they will earn on their savings.

4. _____ (30 minutes) Begin the discussion of **Answer These Questions!**

1. Look up *Genesis 41:34-36* and *Proverbs 30:24-25*. What do you think these passages say about saving?

Genesis 41:34-36 — [Joseph saved during a time of plenty to prepare for a coming famine.]

Proverbs 30:24-25 — [Ants are wise because they save.]

2 How will you begin to save if you are not yet saving?

3 If you have put money into a savings account, the bank will pay you *interest*. How would you describe what *interest* is?

[Interest is the money you are paid by a bank to put your money into a savings account.]

4 Read *Proverbs 21:5*. According to this verse, what is a benefit of saving regularly?

[You will prosper if you save regularly.]

5 How would you define gambling?

[Gambling is defined as playing games of chance for money, betting and taking great risks.]

6 What are some of the different ways people gamble?

[Some of today's more common forms of gambling are casino wagering, betting on sporting events, horse races, dog races and state-run lotteries.]

7 Why do you think most people gamble?

[Most people gamble because they want to get rich quick and to get something for nothing. Many want to become wealthy so they can quit working.]

8 Do you think gambling pleases the Lord? Why?

[Gambling does not please the Lord, because it is contrary to biblical principles.]

Remaining agenda:

1. _____ (5 minutes) Review what the students are required to do for the next chapter.

   - ✓ Read Chapter 10 — Friends.
   - ✓ Answer the Questions on pages 86 and 87.
   - ✓ Memorize *1 Timothy 4:12*.
   - ✓ Complete the **Work It Out!** exercise of writing down some ways to spend money more wisely.

2. _____ (10 minutes) Note in the Prayer Lists requests and answers to prayers.

3. End in prayer.

FRIENDS
Leader's Guide for Chapter 10

Compass's overview of Chapter 10: In this class we explore the importance of selecting good friends and partiality.

Agenda:

1. Open in prayer.

2. _____ (5 minutes) Have everyone recite from memory:

"Let no one look down on your youthfulness, but rather in speech, conduct, love, faith and purity show yourself an example to those who believe" (1 Timothy 4:12).

3. Confirm that everyone has completed the **Let's Get Practical!** exercise of writing down some ways to spend wisely.

4. _____ (30 minutes) Begin the discussion of the **Answer These Questions!**

1 According to *1 Corinthians 15:33*, do our friends influence us? Why do you think it is important to have godly friends?

[Our friends have a big influence on us — either for good or bad.]

2 How can your friends help you handle money wisely?

42

3 Read *1 Timothy 4:12*. What does this verse say about how you should be an example?

[In all areas of life, young people should model godly living.]

4 What are some of the ways you can be an example in handling money in a way that pleases the Lord?

5 Look up the word *partiality* in the dictionary. Write down what you think it means.

[Favoring one person over another.]

6 Read *Leviticus 19:15* and *James 2:1-9*. What do these passages say about partiality (having favorites)?

Leviticus 19:15 — [Do not be partial to the poor or to the great.]

James 2:1-9 — [Do not choose friends because they have a lot of money. It is sin to be partial.]

7 Do you choose friends because they have a lot of money, are popular or are good looking?

8. Look up *Romans 12:16* and *Philippians 2:3*. How do you think each of these verses will help you overcome partiality?

[Be of the same mind toward each other and consider other people as more important than yourself.]

Remaining agenda:

1. _____ (5 minutes) Review what the students are required to do for the next chapter.

   - Read Chapter 11 — How Much Is in the Jars?

   - Answer the Questions on pages 93 to 95.

   - Memorize *Philippians 4:11-13*.

   - Complete the **Work It Out!** exercise of eating more wisely by writing down any junk food you eat and what would be healthier to eat.

2. _____ (10 minutes) Note in the Prayer Lists requests and answers to prayers.

3. End in prayer.

HOW MUCH IS IN THE JARS?
Leader's Guide for Chapter 11

Compass's overview of Chapter 11: This class concentrates on helping the students learn to be content. This is expecially difficult in our culture.

Agenda:

1. Open in prayer.

2. _____ (5 minutes) Have everyone recite from memory:

"For I have learned to be content in whatever circumstances I am. I know how to get along with humble means, and I also know how to live in prosperity ... I can do all things through Him who strengthens me" (Philippians 4:11-13).

3. Confirm that everyone has completed the **Let's Get Practical!** exercise.

4. _____ (35 minutes) Begin the discussion of **Answer These Questions!**

1 Look up the word *contentment* in the dictionary? Write down what you think it means.

[An inner peace that accepts what God has chosen for us in our current circumstances; being happy with what we have.]

2 What do *Luke 3:14, Philippians 4:11-13, 1 Timothy 6:6-8*, and *Hebrews 13:5-6* have to say about contentment?

Luke 3:14 — [We should be content with our income. This does not mean that we should not make an effort to earn more, but that our attitude should be one of contentment.]

Philippians 4:11-13 — [We should be content in any situation.]

1 Timothy 6:6-8 — [Godliness with contentment is a means of great gain. We cannot take anything with us when we die, and we should be content with having our basic needs satisfied.]

Hebrews 13:5-6 — [Because the Lord is our Protector and Provider, we can be content.]

3 Name some things that can make you discontent:

4 Read *1 Corinthians 3:16-17*. If you have asked Jesus Christ into your life, where does God live?

[He lives in you.]

5 Since you are a temple that God lives in, how should you take care of your body?

[We should do a good job of taking care of our bodies by eating good food, exercising regularly and getting enough sleep.]

6 How do you think that eating nutritious food, exercising and getting enough sleep might save you money in the future?

[Trying to stay healthy will help you save money on some expenses like doctors' bills.]

Remaining agenda:

1. _____ (5 minutes) Review what the students are required to do for the next chapter.

   - ✓ Read Chapter 12 — The Secret Discovered.
   - ✓ Answer the Questions on pages 102 and 103.
   - ✓ Memorize *Mark 8:36*.
   - ✓ Complete the **Work It Out!** exercise of writing down the things three ads are selling and how the ads are trying to get you to spend money.

2. Ask your students to be thinking about a "long-term" prayer request for the last class.

3. _____ (10 minutes) Note in the Prayer List requests and answers to prayers.

4. End in prayer.

THE SECRET DISCOVERED
Leader's Guide for Chapter 12

Compass's overview of Chapter 12: This chapter deals with taxes and how understanding eternity should impact how we spend money. Thank the students for their effort in the study.

Agenda:

1. Open in prayer.

2. _____ (5 minutes) Have everyone recite from memory:

"For what does it profit a man to gain the whole world, and forfeit his soul?" (Mark 8:36).

3. Confirm that everyone has completed the **Work It Out!** exercise of writing down the things three ads are selling and the tricks they use to get you to spend money.

4. _____ (30 minutes) Begin the discussion of the **Answer These Questions!**

1. What are taxes? [Taxes are money we pay the government so it can provide services.]

2. Read *Matthew 22:17-21* and *Romans 13:1-7*. Do you think the Lord wants us to pay the government taxes that we owe them? Why?

[Yes, we are required to pay taxes so the government can serve the people.]

51

3 How would you define *eternity*? [Eternity is forever.]

4 Moses was rich when he was growing up. Read *Hebrews 11:24-26*. Why do you think Moses chose to suffer rather than to remain rich?

[Moses was looking forward to receiving God's reward and blessing.]

5 Do you think Moses will be happy in heaven because he made this decision? Why?

[Yes, Moses will be happy because he did what God wanted him to do. He will be able to enjoy the Lord forever in heaven.]

6 Look up *Mark 8:36*. What do you think this verse means?

[A person can get rich or famous, but it means nothing apart from knowing Jesus Christ.]

7 Describe the most helpful part of this entire study to you.

Remind the Students: When you become a teenager, we recommend that you enroll in the Compass *Give, Save & Spend* study for high school students. This will help you with the money issues you will face at this stage of life.

Remaining agenda:

1. (10 minutes) Take prayer requests and note them on the Prayer Lists.

2. End in prayer.

Reminder for leaders:

We suggest you write each student an encouraging letter summarizing what you appreciate most about them. May the Lord richly bless you in every way for your equipping these young people to handle money from a biblical perspective.

HOW TO CONDUCT THE STUDY ONE-ON-ONE

This section is for a parent or any leader who wants to teach the study one-on-one.

1. **Before beginning the study the leader should:**

   - Review the first nine page of this Leader's Guide.
   - Meet with the student to review the course requirements.

2. **Before each class the leader should:**

   - Review the material for that chapter in the Leader's Guide.
   - Memorize the assigned Scripture.
   - Answer the questions in the Leader's Guide.
   - Remember to pray daily for your student.

3. **How to conduct the class:**

Each of the twelve lessons is conducted in the same way. Turn in the Leader's Guide to the chapter and follow the agenda. Use this procedure when teaching one-on-one:

- Open with prayer.
- Recite the scripture that was assigned to be memorized.
- Confirm that the **Work It Out!** exercise has been completed.
- Conduct the **Answer These Questions!** discussion, proceeding as follows:

  - Read any Scriptures under question Number 1.
  - Ask the student to answer all the questions under Number 1.
  - The leader should then answer the questions under Number 1. After answering the questions the leader should then initiate dialogue to make certain the student understands the issue under discussion.
  - Repeat this procedure for question number 2, then question number 3, etc.

- Complete the items listed in the Remaining Agenda in consecutive order.
- Share prayer requests and write them on the Prayer Lists.
- End in prayer.

HOW TO CONDUCT THE STUDY IN A SMALL GROUP

This section is for leaders who are leading the study in a small group setting.

1. **Before starting the study the leader should:**

    ✓ Review the first nine pages of this Leader's Guide.

    ✓ Meet with the students to review the course requirements.

2. **Before each class the leader should:**

    ✓ Review the material for that chapter in the Leader's Guide.

    ✓ Memorize the assigned Scripture.

    ✓ Answer the questions in the Leader's Guide.

    ✓ Remember to pray daily for your students.

3. **How to conduct the class:**

Each of the twelve classes is conducted in the same way. Turn in the Leader's Guide to the appropriate chapter and follow the agenda. Use this procedure when teaching a small group:

   ✓ Open with prayer.

   ✓ The students recite the scripture that was assigned to be memorized.

   ✓ Confirm that students have completed the **Work It Out!** exercise.

   ✓ Conduct the **Answer These Questions!** group discussion, proceeding as follows:

   ■ Assign a student to read any scriptures under question number 1.

   ■ Proceed in a circle asking every person to answer question number 1.

   ■ The leader should then answer the question under number 1. After answering the question the leader should then initiate dialogue to make certain the students understand the principle under discussion.

   ■ Repeat this procedure for question number 2, then question number 3, etc. Start with a different student each time so no one feels singled out.

- ✓ Complete the items listed in the Remaining Agenda in consecutive order.

- ✓ Share prayer requests and write them in the Prayer Lists.

- ✓ End in prayer.

Classroom Dynamics

The most effective group discussions involve group interaction and member-to-member participation.

- ✓ In diagram 1 the sole focus is on the teacher, who does all the talking. The students are passive. This is **not** how the Compass Study is designed to be taught.

- ✓ Diagram 2 reflects the people in a group interacting with one another and a leader who guides and facilitates the discussion. The leader must establish an environment in which students have the freedom to express their insights and questions.

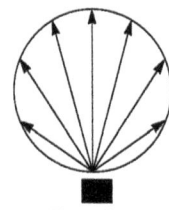
Leader
Diagram 1 — The Incorrect Method

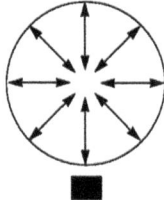
Leader
Diagram 2 — The Correct Method

HOW TO CONDUCT THE STUDY IN SUNDAY SCHOOL

> This section is for teachers who are leading the study in a Sunday school setting.

1. **Before beginning the study the teacher should:**

    - Review the first nine pages of this Leader's Guide.

    - Meet with students to review the course requirements.

2. **Before each class the teacher should:**

    - Review the material for that lesson in the Leader's Guide.

    - Memorize the assigned Scripture.

    - Answer the questions in the Leader's Guide.

    - Pray daily for your students.

3. **How to conduct the class:**

Each of the twelve lessons is conducted in the same way. Turn in the Leader's Guide to the appropriate chapter and follow the agenda. Use this procedure when teaching in a Sunday school:

- Open with prayer.

- The students recite the Scripture that was assigned to be memorized. This can be done by each student in front of the entire class or by the entire class in unison — depending upon the size of the class.

- Conduct the group discussion. The discussion should proceed as follows:

    - Assign a child to read the scriptures under question number 1.

    - Ask four or five students to answer all questions under number 1.

    - The teacher should then answer the questions under number 1. After answering the questions, the teacher should initiate further dialogue to make certain the students understand the issues under discussion.

    - Repeat this procedure for question number 2, then question number 3, etc. Start with a different student each time so no one feels singled out.

- Complete the items listed in the Remaining Agenda in consecutive order.

- Break up into prayer groups of four to eight people, share prayer requests and write them in the Prayer Lists.

- End in prayer.

Classroom Dynamics

The most effective group discussions involve group interaction and member-to-member participation.

- In diagram 1 the sole focus is on the teacher, who does all the talking. The students are passive. This is **not** how the Compass Study is designed to be taught.

- Diagram 2 reflects the people in a class interacting with one another and a leader who guides and facilitates the discussion. The teacher must establish an environment in which students have the freedom to express their insights and questions.

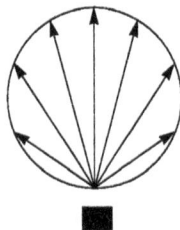

Leader
Diagram 1 — The Incorrect Method

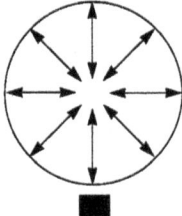

Leader
Diagram 2 — The Correct Method

HOW TO CONDUCT THE STUDY IN SCHOOL

This section is for teachers who are leading the study in a school setting.

1. **What the teacher should know:**

This study is designed for both Christian schools and home schools.

On the following 24 pages are 12 quizzes you can use. Each chapter has one quiz with the answers for the teacher and one test without the answers for the students. Please photocopy as many of the student quizzes as you need.

Should you choose to develop your own quiz, you may use any of the questions contained on the enclosed tests.

2. **Before beginning the study the teacher should:**

    - Review the first nine pages of this Leader's Guide.

    - Meet with students to review the course requirements.

3. **If possible, divide into groups of seven or eight.** If the class has more than eight students, we recommend that you divide into smaller groups of no more than eight students. This will be possible only if you have a teacher for each group. Smaller groups allow the children to be more actively involved and more attentive.

4. **Before each lesson the teacher should:**

    - Review the material for that chapter in the Leader's Guide.

    - Memorize the assigned scripture.

    - Answer the questions in the Leader's Guide.

    - Pray daily for your students.

5. **How to conduct the class**

Each of the twelve lessons is conducted in the same way. Turn in the Leader's Guide to the appropriate chapter and follow the agenda. Use this procedure when teaching in a school:

    - Open with prayer.

    - The students recite the scripture that was assigned to be memorized. This can be done by each student in front of the entire class or by the entire class in unison.

- ✓ Conduct the group discussion. The discussion should proceed as follows:

    - ■ Assign a student to read any scriptures under question Number 1.

    - ■ Ask four or five students to answer question Number 1.

    - ■ The teacher should then answer question Number 1. After answering the question, the teacher should initiate further dialogue to make certain the students understand the issues under discussion.

    - ■ Repeat this procedure for question Number 2, then question Number 3, etc.

- ✓ Complete the items listed in the Remaining Agenda (found in the Leader's Guide) in consecutive order.

- ✓ Break up into prayer groups of four to eight people, share prayer requests, and write them in the Prayer Lists.

- ✓ End in prayer.

Classroom Dynamics

The most effective group discussions involve group interaction and member-to-member participation.

- ✓ In diagram 1 the sole focus is on the teacher, who does all the talking. The students are passive. This is **not** how the Compass Study is designed to be taught.

- ✓ Diagram 2 reflects the people in a class interacting with one another and a leader who guides and facilitates the discussion. The teacher must establish an environment in which students have the freedom to express their insights and questions.

Leader
Diagram 1 — The Incorrect Method

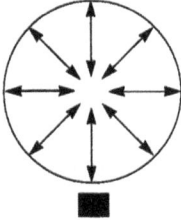
Leader
Diagram 2 — The Correct Method

Q U I Z
Chapter 1 — Teacher's Edition

1. Write out *Luke 16:11*.

   If therefore you have not been faithful in the use of worldly wealth, who will entrust the true riches to you?

2. God's way of handling money is different from the way most people handle money.

   ❏ **True**   ❏ False

3. What is the biggest difference between the way most people handle money and God's way?

   The biggest difference is that most people think that God has nothing to do with handling money. Yet Scripture tells us He plays a big part.

4. Circle the number of verses in the Bible that talk about money.

   550   (**2,350**)

   1,250   10,750

5. Write out why you think the Bible says so much about money.

QUIZ
Chapter 1

1. Write out *Luke 16:11*. _____

2. God's way of handling money is different from the way most people handle money.

    ❏ True   ❏ False

3. What is the biggest difference between the way most people handle money and God's way? _____

4. Circle the number of verses in the Bible that talk about money.

    550   2,350

    1,250   10,750

5. Write out why you think the Bible says so much about money.

Q U I Z
Chapter 2 — Teacher's Edition

1. Write out *1 Chronicles 29:11-12*:
   Everything in the heavens and earth is yours, O Lord, and this is your kingdom. We adore you as being in control of everything. Riches and honor come from you alone, and you are the ruler of all mankind; your hand controls power and might, and it is at your discretion that men are made great and given strength.

2. God is the owner of everything you have.

   ❏ **True**   ❏ False

3. Who controls everything that happens?
   God.

4. God promises to provide the following needs.
   Food and clothing.

5. Give an example from the Bible of the Lord providing needs.
   Elijah; Jesus feeding the 5,000 and 4,000; to name a few.

6. God owns your things. Write down how understanding this will help you.

Q U I Z
Chapter 2

1. Write out *1 Chronicles 29:11-12*: _____

2. God is the owner of everything you have.

   ❏ True   ❏ False

3. Who controls everything that happens? _____

4. God promises to provide the following needs.

5. Give an example from the Bible of the Lord providing needs.

6. God owns your things. Write down how understanding this will help you.

Q U I Z
Chapter 3 — Teacher's Edition

1. Write down *1 Corinthians 4:2*.
   Moreover it is required in stewards, that a man be found faithful.

2. How would you define a *steward*?
   A steward is a manager or overseer of someone else's property.

3. Circle our major responsibility with money.

   To get rich (**To be faithful**)

   To have a nice home   To drive a new car

4. God knows everything about you and sees everything you do. How will understanding this change what you do?

5. *Luke 16:12* says, "And if you have not been faithful with that which is another's, who will give you that which is your own?" According to this verse, why do you think some people don't get more things?
   Because they have not been faithful with another's possessions.

6. Write down why you think it is important to be faithful with small things.

QUIZ
Chapter 3

1. Write down *1 Corinthians 4:2*. _____
_____
_____

2. How would you define a *steward*? _____
_____
_____

3. Circle our major responsibility with money.

    To get rich   To be faithful

    To have a nice home   To drive a new car

4. God knows everything about you and sees everything you do. How will understanding this change what you do? _____
_____
_____

5. *Luke 16:12* says, "And if you have not been faithful with that which is another's, who will give you that which is your own?" According to this verse, why do you think some people don't get more things?
_____
_____
_____

6. Write down why you think it is important to be faithful with small things.
_____
_____
_____
_____
_____
_____
_____

Q U I Z
Chapter 4 — Teacher's Edition

1. Write out *Proverbs 22:7*.
   Just as the rich rule the poor, so the borrower is servant to the lender.

2. Define *debt*.
   Money that one person is obligated to pay to another.

3. Circle what the Bible says about debt.

    The more debt you have, the better.

    (**We should try to stay out of debt.**)

    Everybody should go into debt.

4. Define *interest*.
   Interest is the extra money you pay when you borrow money.

5. Write down why you think the Lord wants us to stay out of debt.

QUIZ
Chapter 4

1. Write out *Proverbs 22:7*: _____
   _____
   _____

2. Define *debt*: _____
   _____
   _____

3. Circle what the Bible says about debt.

   The more debt you have, the better.

   We should try to stay out of debt.

   Everybody should go into debt.

4. Define *interest*. _____
   _____
   _____

5. Write down why you think the Lord wants us to stay out of debt.
   _____
   _____
   _____
   _____
   _____
   _____

Q U I Z
Chapter 5 — Teacher's Edition

1. Write *Proverbs 12:15*:
   The way of a fool is right in his own eyes, but a wise man is he who listens to counsel.

2. Define *counsel*.
   Seeking the advice of another.

3. Explain the reason for seeking counsel.
   We seek counsel to get suggestions that can help us make good decisions.

4. The Bible should be a source of counsel.

   ❏ **True**   ❏ False

5. Circle those who should *not* be your counselors.

   parents   (**wicked people**)   pastors

   experienced people   (**a fortune-teller**)

6. Write down how you think you should seek the counsel of the Lord?
   Primarily through the study of the Bible and prayer.

QUIZ
Chapter 5

1. Write out *Proverbs 12:15*. _____
   _____
   _____

2. Define *counsel*. _____
   _____
   _____

3. Explain the reason for seeking counsel. _____
   _____
   _____

4. The Bible should be a source of counsel.

   ❏ True   ❏ False

5. Circle those who should *not* be your counselors.

   parents   wicked people   pastors

   experienced people   a fortune-teller

6. Write down how you think you should seek the counsel of the Lord?
   _____
   _____
   _____
   _____
   _____
   _____

QUIZ
Chapter 6 — Teacher's Edition

1. Write out *Leviticus 19:11*.
   You shall not steal, nor deal falsely, nor lie to one another.

2. Circle why the Lord wants us to be honest in small things.

   It is easier to get caught.

   (If we are not honest in small things, we will not be honest in big things.)

3. Define *restitution*.
   Restitution is the return of property that was acquired dishonestly, with some extra besides.

4. What should you do if you steal something?
   Return that which was stolen.

5. Write down why you think the Lord wants us to always be honest.

Q U I Z
Chapter 6

1. Write out *Leviticus 19:11*. _____
   _____
   _____

2. Circle why the Lord wants us to be honest in small things.

   It is easier to get caught.

   If we are not honest in small things,
   we will not be honest in big things.

3. Define *restitution*.
   _____
   _____
   _____

4. What should you do if you steal something? _____
   _____
   _____

5. Write down why you think the Lord wants us to always be honest.
   _____
   _____
   _____
   _____
   _____
   _____

QUIZ
Chapter 7 — Teacher's Edition

1. Write out *Acts 20:35*:
   Remember the words of the Lord Jesus, that He Himself said, "It is more blessed to give than to receive."

2. Attitudes are important in giving. What should our attitude be when giving.
   We should be loving, cheerful givers.

3. How can you give with the right attitude?
   Give each gift to Jesus Christ because you love Him and are thankful for all He has done.

4. It is more blessed to give than to receive.

   ❏ **True**   ❏ False

5. Define a *tithe*.
   A tithe is 10 percent of our income.

7. Write down what the Bible says about giving to the poor.

QUIZ
Chapter 7

1. Write out *Acts 20:35*. _____
   _____
   _____

2. Attitudes are important in giving. What should our attitude be when giving? _____
   _____
   _____

3. How can you give with the right attitude? _____
   _____
   _____

4. It is more blessed to give than to receive.

   ❑ True ❑ False

5. Define a *tithe*. _____
   _____
   _____

7. Write down what the Bible says about giving to the poor.
   _____
   _____
   _____
   _____
   _____
   _____

QUIZ
Chapter 8 — Teacher's Edition

1. Write out *Colossians 3:23-24*.

   Whatever you do, do your work heartily, as for the Lord rather than for men ... It is the Lord Christ whom you serve.

2. Circle whom you really work for.

   My parents   (**Jesus Christ**)

   My boss   My teacher

3. Circle the parts that God plays in your work.

   (**He gives us skills.**)   He does our homework.

   He studies hard for tests.   (**He promotes us.**)

   (**He gives success.**)   He does our work.

4. Write down what the Bible says about hard work and laziness.

Q U I Z
Chapter 8

1. Write out *Colossians 3:23-24*. _____
   _____
   _____

2. Circle whom you really work for.

   My parents   Jesus Christ

   My boss   My teacher

3. Circle the parts that God plays in your work.

   He gives us skills.   He does our homework.

   He studies hard for tests. He promotes us.

   He gives success.   He does our work.

4. Write down what the Bible says about hard work and laziness.
   _____
   _____
   _____
   _____
   _____
   _____

Q U I Z
Chapter 9 — Teacher's Edition

1. Write out *Proverbs 21:20* and *Proverbs 21:5*.

   The wise man saves for the future, but the foolish man spends whatever he gets (*Proverbs 21:20*). **Steady plodding brings prosperity; hasty speculation brings poverty** (*Proverbs 21:5*).

2. What does the Bible say about saving?

   The word of God encourages saving.

3. Circle the creature the Bible honors for saving.

   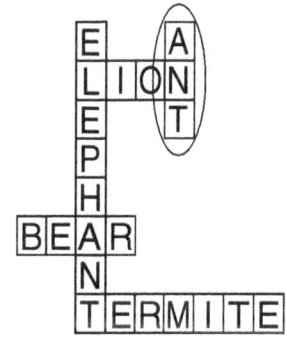

4. The bank pays you interest on your savings.

   ❏ **True** ❏ False

5. What does the Bible say about gambling?

   Gambling is discouraged, because it does not develop character or enable a person to benefit from hard work.

6. Explain how a person can come to know Jesus Christ as their Savior and Lord.

QUIZ
Chapter 9

1. Write out *Proverbs 21:20* and *Proverbs 21:5*. _____
   _____
   _____

2. What does the Bible say about saving? _____
   _____
   _____
   _____

3. Circle the creature the Bible honors for saving.

   ```
         A
   E    N
   L I O N
   E    T
   P
   H
   B E A R
   N
   T E R M I T E
   ```

4. The bank pays you interest on your savings.

   ❏ True   ❏ False

5. What does the Bible say about gambling? _____
   _____
   _____
   _____

6. Explain how a person can come to know Jesus Christ as their Savior and Lord. _____
   _____
   _____
   _____
   _____
   _____

QUIZ
Chapter 10 — Teacher's Edition

1. Write out *1 Timothy 4:12* in its entirety:
   Let no one look down on your youthfulness, but rather in speech, conduct, love, faith and purity, show yourself an example to those who believe.

2. Why is it important to have godly friends?
   Because we are deeply influenced by our friends and peers.

3. How can you help others to handle money wisely?

4. How would you define *partiality*?
   Partiality is liking someone because he or she is popular or has a lot of money.

5. Describe how you plan to get a group of godly friends that you become close to.

QUIZ
Chapter 10

1. Write out *1 Timothy 4:12*. _____

2. Why is it important to have godly friends? _____

3. How can you help others to handle money wisely? _____

4. How would you define *partiality*? _____

5. Describe how you plan to get a group of godly friends that you become close to. _____

QUIZ
Chapter 11 — Teacher's Edition

1. Write out *Philippians 4:11-13*.

   For I have learned to be content in whatever circumstances I am. I know how to get along with humble means, and I also know how to live in prosperity...I can do all things through Him who strengthens me.

2. Define *contentment*.

   Contentment means we are happy with what the Lord has given us at this time.

3. Circle the things that can make us discontented.

The Bible	**(Magazine ads)**
(Television commercials)	**(Friends)**
Prayer	The Lord

4. If you have asked Jesus Christ into your life, where does He live?

   He lives in you.

5. Why should I take good care of my body?

   Because I am a temple of God. It will also probably save me money because I will stay healthier.

6. Describe what God says about contentment.

QUIZ
Chapter 11

1. Write out *Philippians 4:11-13*. _____
   _____
   _____

2. Define *contentment*. _____
   _____
   _____
   _____

3. Circle the things that can make us discontented.

   The Bible   Magazine ads

   Television commercials Friends

   Prayer   The Lord

4. If you have asked Jesus Christ into your life, where does He live?
   _____
   _____
   _____

5. Why should I take good care of my body? _____
   _____
   _____

6. Describe what God says about contentment. _____
   _____
   _____
   _____
   _____
   _____

Q U I Z
Chapter 12 — Teacher's Edition

1. Write out *Mark 8:36*.

    For what does it profit a man to gain the whole world, and forfeit his soul?

2. What are *taxes*?

    Taxes are money we pay the government so it can provide services.

3. The Bible says we should pay taxes we owe.

    ❑ **True**   ❑ False

4. How would you define *eternity*?

    Eternity is forever.

5. Circle the right answers.

    How we spend money on earth will make —

    No difference in heaven

    (A big difference for me in heaven)

    (A big difference for others in heaven)

6. Describe the biggest lesson you learned from reading *The Secret*.

QUIZ
Chapter 12

1. Write out *Mark 8:36*. _____
_____

2. What are *taxes*? _____
_____
_____

3. The Bible says we should pay taxes we owe.

    ❏ True   ❏ False

4. How would you define *eternity*? _____
_____
_____

5. Circle the right answers.

    How we spend money on earth will make —

    No difference in heaven

    A big difference for me in heaven

    A big difference for others in heaven

6. Describe the biggest lesson you learned from reading *The Secret*.
_____
_____
_____
_____
_____
_____

PRAYER LIST

Name: _____ School: _____

Telephone: _____ Text: _____

Home Address: _____ Age: _____

_____ Social Media: _____

_____ Parents: _____

Chapter	Pray For Me	Answers To Prayer
1		
2		
3		
4		
5		
6		
7		
8		
9		
10		
11		
12		

"Pray for one another" James 5:16

PRAYER LIST

Name: _____ School: _____
Telephone: _____ Text: _____
Home Address: _____ Age: _____
_____ Social Media: _____
_____ Parents: _____

Chapter	Pray For Me	Answers To Prayer
1		
2		
3		
4		
5		
6		
7		
8		
9		
10		
11		
12		

"Pray for one another" James 5:16

PRAYER LIST

Name: _____ School: _____

Telephone: _____ Text: _____

Home Address: _____ Age: _____

_____ Social Media: _____

_____ Parents: _____

Chapter	Pray For Me	Answers To Prayer
1		
2		
3		
4		
5		
6		
7		
8		
9		
10		
11		
12		

"Pray for one another" James 5:16

PRAYER LIST

Name: _____ School: _____
Telephone: _____ Text: _____
Home Address: _____ Age: _____
_____ Social Media: _____
_____ Parents: _____

Chapter	Pray For Me	Answers To Prayer
1		
2		
3		
4		
5		
6		
7		
8		
9		
10		
11		
12		

"Pray for one another" James 5:16

PRAYER LIST

Name: _____ School: _____
Telephone: _____ Text: _____
Home Address: _____ Age: _____
_____   Social Media: _____
_____   Parents: _____

Chapter	Pray For Me	Answers To Prayer
1		
2		
3		
4		
5		
6		
7		
8		
9		
10		
11		
12		

"Pray for one another" James 5:16

PRAYER LIST

Name: _____ School: _____
Telephone: _____ Text: _____
Home Address: _____ Age: _____
_____ Social Media: _____
_____ Parents: _____

Chapter	Pray For Me	Answers To Prayer
1		
2		
3		
4		
5		
6		
7		
8		
9		
10		
11		
12		

"Pray for one another" James 5:16

PRAYER LIST

Name: _____ School: _____
Telephone: _____ Text: _____
Home Address: _____ Age: _____
_____ Social Media: _____
_____ Parents: _____

Chapter	Pray For Me	Answers To Prayer
1		
2		
3		
4		
5		
6		
7		
8		
9		
10		
11		
12		

"Pray for one another" James 5:16

PRAYER LIST

Name: _____ School: _____
Telephone: _____ Text: _____
Home Address: _____ Age: _____
_____ Social Media: _____
_____ Parents: _____

Chapter	Pray For Me	Answers To Prayer
1		
2		
3		
4		
5		
6		
7		
8		
9		
10		
11		
12		

"Pray for one another" James 5:16

We hope you enjoy this book from Moody Publishers.
Our goal is to provide high-quality, thought-provoking books
and products that connect truth to your real needs and challenges.
For more information on other books and products
written and produced from a biblical perspective,
go to www.moodypublishers.com or write to:

Moody Publishers
820 N. LaSalle Boulevard
Chicago, IL 60610